MEASURING WEIGHT

By Julia Vogel • Illustrated by Luanne Marten

The Child's World®

Published by The Child's World®
1980 Lookout Drive • Mankato, MN 56003-1705
800-599-READ • www.childsworld.com

Acknowledgments
The Child's World®: Mary Berendes, Publishing Director
The Design Lab: Cover and interior design
Amnet: Cover and interior production
Red Line Editorial: Editorial direction

Photo credits
Igor Stepovik/Shutterstock Images, cover, 1; Olga Popova/Shutterstock Images,
cover, 1, 2; Anna Omelchenko/Shutterstock Images, 5; Mandy Godbehear/
Shutterstock Images, 6; iStockphoto, 11, 16; Shutterstock Images, 12; Eric Isselée/
Shutterstock Images, 19

ISBN 9781614732846
LCCN 2012933674

Printed in the United States of America
Mankato, MN
July 2012
PA02121

ABOUT THE AUTHOR
Award-winning author Julia Vogel carried lots of heavy books while studying for degrees in biology and forestry. Julia has four kids—Nathan is the heaviest—and three cats—Sweetheart is the lightest.

ABOUT THE ILLUSTRATOR
Luanne Marten has been drawing for a long time. She earned a bachelor's degree in art and design from the University of Kansas. Probably the heaviest thing she has drawn is the world, or at least a globe.

TABLE OF CONTENTS

Heavy or Light?

Who has the heaviest backpack? Who has the lightest lunch? Which book weighs the most?

How can you find the answers? By measuring weight! Weight is how heavy something or someone is.

How can you tell how heavy your backpack is? By weighing it!

When you throw a ball, **gravity** is what causes it to fall to the ground.

Gravity's Effect

What causes something or someone to be heavy or light? Earth has a force called gravity. Gravity pulls all things toward Earth. Weight is a measurement of Earth's gravity on objects.

You feel gravity whenever you jump up. No matter how hard you try to stay up, you come down! Gravity is stronger on heavier objects.

Comparing Weights

People haven't always had tools for measuring weight. Instead they measured weight by comparing two or more objects.

You can compare the weights of two books from your backpack. Hold one in each hand. Can you tell which one is heavier?

Can you tell which book is heavier just by holding the books in your hands?

Balancing Act

A **balance** is a good tool for comparing weight. It works like a seesaw on the playground. What happens if a big brother sits on one end and his little sister sits on the other? The sister goes up. That is because gravity pulls the boy down more. He weighs more.

But if twins sit on each end, they balance. The twins weigh the same amount. The force of gravity is equal on each end.

On this balance, the right side is heavier than the left.

Your doctor checks your weight to make sure you are healthy.

TYPES OF SCALES

What tool should you use to measure weight? That depends on what you're measuring. Spring scales are good for bags of apples at the store. Kitchen scales help measure how much chocolate to put into the candy you're making. Bathroom scales measure people's weights. Truck scales measure trucks, cars, and even elephants.

Ounces and Pounds

A balance is good for comparing, but you can't find out how much something weighs. You have to use a scale for that. Many scales measure weight in the **units** of ounces and pounds.

Small, light things, such as a slice of bread, are measured in ounces. Sixteen ounces are in 1 pound. If you have a 1-pound loaf of bread and cut it into 16 equal slices, each slice weighs 1 ounce.

Tons and Tons

What if you had 200 bowling balls to weigh? They would be heavy—about 2,000 pounds. That's about as much as a small car!

For very heavy things, a different unit—the ton—is used. One ton is 2,000 pounds. That means 200 bowling balls weigh about 1 ton. How much would 600 bowling balls weigh? Three tons!

A small car can weigh about 2,000 pounds, or 1 ton.

On average, a cell phone weighs about 130 grams.

METRIC TON

There is a metric ton, too. One metric ton is 1,000 kilograms. A metric ton is not the same as a ton in the **US customary system.** One US ton is 907 kilograms.

Metric System

People in the United States measure weight in ounces, pounds, and tons. These units are part of the US customary system.

But most of the world uses the **metric system**. In the metric system, the basic unit for weight is the gram. A paper clip or a dollar bill weigh about 1 gram.

Kilograms are used to weigh heavier things. One kilogram is 1,000 grams. A heavy schoolbook might weigh about 1 kilogram.

Estimate It

What if you don't have a balance or a scale? You can **estimate**. To estimate a small object, hold something that you know weighs a few ounces, like a nickel, in one hand. Hold the object you're weighing in the other hand. Can you tell if one object is heavier? To estimate a heavy object, use your eyes. Does a rhino look heavier or lighter than a hippo?

You can use tools to check your estimates. For the small object, weigh it on a scale. For the heavy object, use the Internet. Look up how much a rhino and a hippo weigh to find out which weighs more. You'll learn a ton!

You can probably guess which dog weighs more—the one on the right!

Lots of Units

Confused by all the different units for weight? Here's a list to help you keep them straight.

1 pound = 16 ounces

1 ton = 2,000 pounds

1 kilogram = 1,000 grams

1 metric ton = 1,000 kilograms

ADDING WITH UNITS
Make sure you add measurements that have the same units. Two plus two does not equal four if you are adding tons and ounces. Remember to add pounds to pounds, ounces to ounces, and so on.

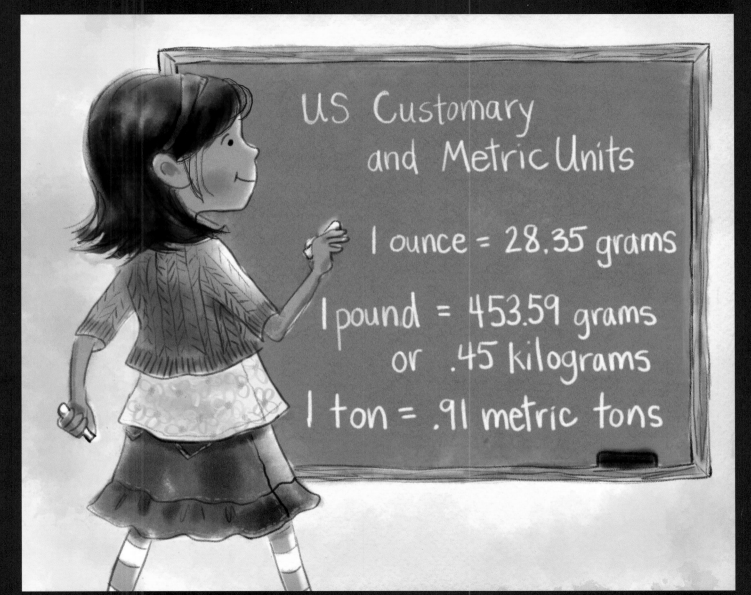

Practice learning the US customary and metric units.

Measuring Mania

Now you can answer questions by weighing. You can tell in pounds and grams who has the heaviest backpack, the lightest lunch, and the weightiest books.

What other questions can you answer? Grab your scales and start measuring!

What will you weigh today?

Glossary

balance (BAL-uhns): A balance is a tool used for comparing weights of things. You can use a balance to see which of two objects is heavier.

estimate (ES-tuh-mate): To estimate means to make an educated guess to find out the value, amount, or distance of something. You can estimate weights if you don't have a balance or a scale.

gravity (GRAV-i-tee): Gravity is the force that pulls objects toward another object. Gravity helps give things weight.

metric system (MEH-trik SIS-tuhm): The metric system is a system of measuring based on the meter and the kilogram. Most of the world uses the metric system for measuring.

units (YOU-nits): Units are standard amounts used to measure. Pounds and grams are two units used for weight.

US customary system (YOO-es KUS-tuh-mer-ee SIS-tuhm): The US customary system is a system of measuring that uses feet, inches, and miles. Pounds and ounces are weight units used in the US customary system.

Books

Cleary, Brian P. *On the Scale: A Weighty Tale.* Minneapolis, MN: Millbrook Press, 2008.

Kensler, Chris. *Secret Treasures and Magical Measures Revealed: Adventures in Measuring.* New York: Simon & Schuster, 2003.

Schwartz, David M. *Millions to Measure.* New York: HarperCollins, 2003.

Web Sites

Visit our Web site for links about measuring weight: **childsworld.com/links**

Note to Parents, Teachers, and Librarians: We routinely verify our Web links to make sure they are safe and active sites. So encourage your readers to check them out!

Index